JOAN TOWER

STRING FORCE

FOR SOLO VIOLIN

AMP 8318

First Printing: September 2017

ISBN: 978-1-4950-9926-7

Associated Music Publishers, Inc.

DISTRIBUTED BY

HAL•LEONARD®

www.halleonard.com

www.musicsalesclassical.com

*Commissioned by
the International Violin Competition of Indianapolis
for the 2010 Competition*

*Underwritten by the Christel DeHaan Family Foundation
in honor of the children and families of Christel House.*

*First performance: 10 September 2010
Contestants of the 2010 International Violin Competition of Indianapolis*

Composer Note:

String Force (2010) was commissioned by the International Violin Competition of Indianapolis for the 2010 Competition and underwritten by the Christel DeHaan Family Foundation in honor of the children and families of Christel House. It is dedicated with great affection and admiration to the violinist Jaime Laredo.

The 7-minute work was an attempt at writing a challenging piece for violin. Between the high speed of notes within a visceral energy context and the high delicate registral writing, there are many technical as well as musical challenges within this work. After hearing the sixteen semi-finalists at the Indianapolis Violin Competition perform *String Force*, I realized there is also much range for interpretation.

I want to thank Ida and Ani Kavafian and Maria Bachmann for their help in the technical challenges of writing for violin.

— Joan Tower

duration circa 7 minutes

Information on Joan Tower and her works is available on musicsalesclassical.com

dedicated with love to Jaime Laredo

STRING FORCE

Joan Tower

2

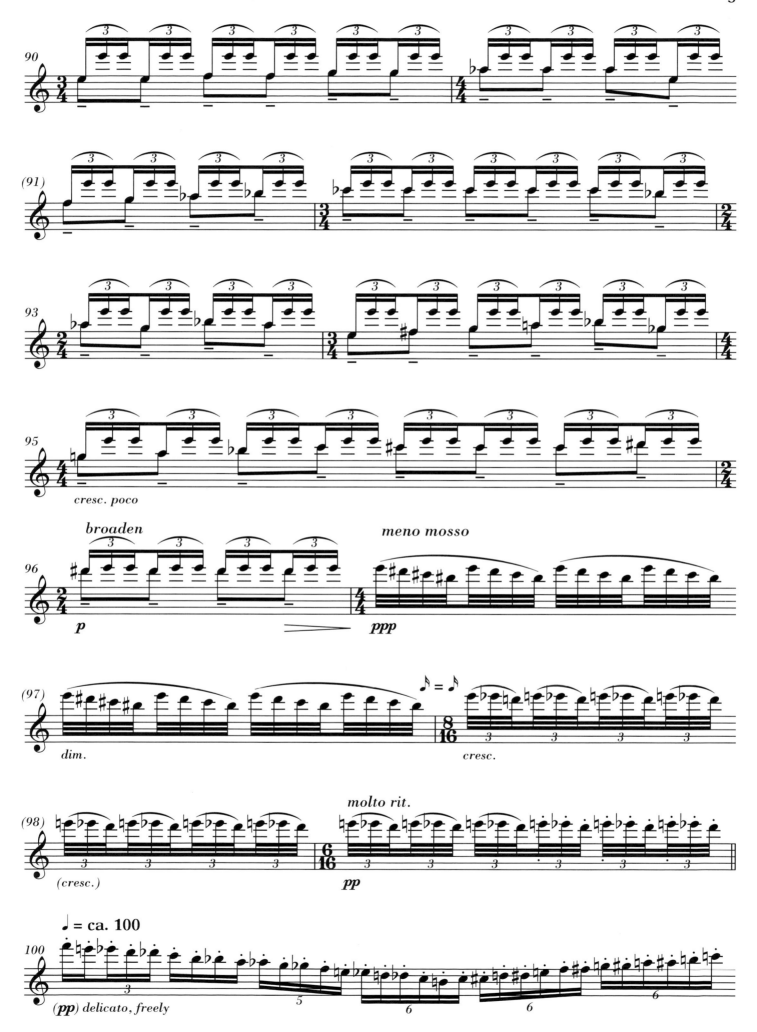